Oktoberfest Recipes for the German Beer Festival

About the Author

Laura Sommers is The Recipe Lady!

She is the #1 Best Selling Author of over 80 recipe books.

She is a loving wife and mother who lives on a small farm in Baltimore County, Maryland and has a passion for all things domestic especially when it comes to saving money. She has a profitable eBay business and is a couponing addict, avid blogger and YouTuber.

Follow her tips and tricks to learn how to make delicious meals on a budget, save money or to learn the latest life hack!

Visit her blog for even more great recipes and to learn which books are **FREE** for download each week:

http://the-recipe-lady.blogspot.com/

Visit her Amazon Author Page to see her latest books:

amazon.com/author/laurasommers

© Copyright 2016. Laura Sommers.
All rights reserved.
No part of this book may be reproduced in any form or by any
electronic or mechanical means without written permission of
the author. All text, illustrations and design are the exclusive
property of
Laura Sommers

About the Author ii

Introduction 1

Oktoberfest Potato Beer Soup...2

Oktoberfest Bratwurst and Sauerkraut 4

Oktoberfest Wiener Schnitzel 5

Oktoberfest Onion Pretzel Rolls 7

Oktoberfest Beer Braised Brisket...9

Oktoberfest Schupfnudeln (Fried Potato Dumplings) 11

Oktoberfest Duck Meatballs...13

Oktoberfest Jaeger Schnitzel...16

Oktoberfest Fried Potatoes with Poached Eggs 18

German Creamed Spinach 20

German Potato Salad..21

German Red Cabbage Soup...22

German Twists 24

German Lebkuchen (Christmas Cookie)..26

Oktoberfest German Honey Cookies 28

Oktoberfest Cut Out Cookies..29

Oktuberfest German Chocolate Cake 30

Oktoberfest Sauerbraten 32

German Gingersnaps 34

Oktoberfest Hoernchen (Christmas Cookies) 35

Oktuberfest Soft Pretzels 37

German Beer Festival Kielbasa 38

Oktoberfest Uber-Braten Kielbasa and Sauerkraut Casserole 39

Oktoberfest Cucumber Slices With Dill 41

Oktoberfest Bierocks (Meat Pockets) 42

Bavarian Kaes-Spaetzle (Egg Noodles) 44

German Rouladen (Beef Olive) 45

Oktuberfest Potato Leek Soup 46

Ocotoberfest Boiled Potatoes 47

Oktoberfest Semmelknoedel (Bread Dumplings) 48

Oktoberfest Beer Cheese Dip 50

Oktoberfest Red Cabbage with Apples 51

German Zwiebelkuchen (Onion Pie)..52

German Currywurst 54

German Chicken 55

German Rice...56

Oktoberfest Pork Shank 57

Oktoberfest Sausage and Sauerkraut Fritter...58

Oktoberfest Sauerkraut 60

Oktoberfest Potato Pancakes 61

Oktoberfest Mustardy Cabbage..62

Oktoberfest Beer-Basted Sausage 63

Oktoberfest Apple Strudel 64

Oktoberfest Cherry Kuchen Bars 65

Oktoberfest German Stuffing..66

About the Author 67

Other books in This Series 68

Introduction

Whether you are German or not, Autumn means Oktoberfest, spelled Oktuberfest or Octuberfest in German, and lots of beer, parties and food!

Oktoberfest is the worlds largest beer festival which is called a Volksfest or traveling funfair in Germany. The heart of these celebrations are in Munich, Bavaria, Germany where it is often called the Wiesn, after the colloquial name for the fairgrounds (Theresienwiese), but celebrations happen all over the world. Celebrations start in mid September and run through to October in Munich, however, in other places of the world, it is generally celebrated in October.

This cookbook captures the more traditional German dishes made for the festival and for German food enthusiasts. I hope that you enjoy!

Oktoberfest Potato Beer Soup

Ingredients:

4 cups chicken stock
3 large russet potatoes, peeled and cubed
1 tbsp. Dijon mustard
8 oz. sliced smoked bacon
2 carrots, diced
Kosher salt
Freshly ground pepper
3 stalks celery, diced
2 bay leaves
1 small bundle fresh thyme, tied together with kitchen twine
1 leek, green top trimmed, diced
1 cup light German beer, such as Pilsner
1/4 cup sliced fresh chives

Directions:

1. Combine 2 cups of the chicken stock and one-third of the potatoes in a small saucepan. Bring to a boil, and then reduce to a simmer until fork-tender, 15 to 18 minutes. Stir in the mustard to combine, and then blend to a smooth puree using an immersion or regular blender.
2. Cook the bacon until crispy.
3. Transfer bacon to a paper-towel-lined plate to drain.
4. Drain the bacon fat, reserving 3 tbsps. in the pot.
5. Increase heat to medium-high and add the carrots.
6. Sprinkle with salt and pepper and cook for 3 minutes, and then add the remaining potatoes, celery, bay leaves, leeks and thyme and season with salt and pepper.
7. Cook until the leeks are soft, 4 minutes, and then pour in the beer and bring to a boil until the beer has cooked down to about 2 tbsps., 2 to 4 minutes.
8. Pour in the remaining chicken stock and the reserved potato puree.

9. Stir to combine and bring the mixture to a boil.
10. Reduce to a simmer and cook uncovered until the vegetables are just tender, 6 to 8 minutes.
11. Season with salt and pepper.
12. To serve, ladle the soup into bowls.
13. Crumble the reserved bacon on top and garnish with the chives.
14. Serve and enjoy!

Oktoberfest Bratwurst and Sauerkraut

Ingredients:

2 tbsps. oil
2 pounds fresh bratwurst links
2 onions, chopped
2 garlic cloves, minced
3 cups chicken stock
1 tbsp. paprika
1 tbsp. caraway seed
4 cups sauerkraut, drained
2 tbsps. chopped fresh dill
1 baguette

Directions:

1. In a large pan, heat oil over high heat.
2. Brown bratwurst in oil and reduce heat to medium.
3. Add onions and garlic and cook until lightly caramelized.
4. Add stock, paprika, caraway seeds, and sauerkraut.
5. Simmer for 45 minutes.
6. Remove from heat and stir in fresh dill.
7. Serve on a baguette and enjoy!

Oktoberfest Wiener Schnitzel

Ingredients:

Four 5-oz. veal cutlets, pounded 1/8_inch thick
Kosher salt
Freshly ground pepper
1 cup all-purpose flour
2 tbsps. German hot mustard
3 eggs
2 cups plain dried breadcrumbs
1/2 cup canola oil
1/2 cup unsalted butter
1/4 cup fresh flat-leaf parsley, roughly chopped
1 lemon, cut into wedges

Directions:

1. Place each veal cutlet in between 2 pieces of plastic wrap and pound using the spiky side of a meat mallet. This is not to further flatten the meat, but to tenderize it. Lightly sprinkle with 1/2 tsp. salt and 1/2 tsp. pepper.
2. Set up the breading station. Whisk together the flour, 1/4 tsp. salt and 1/4 tsp. pepper in a shallow baking dish, and whisk together the mustard and eggs in another shallow baking dish. Combine the breadcrumbs with 1/4 tsp. salt and 1/4 tsp. pepper in a third baking dish.
3. Dredge each veal cutlet first in the flour, then through the egg mixture, and lastly through the breadcrumbs. Transfer onto a baking sheet lined with a cooling rack and refrigerate for 15 minutes.
4. Preheat the oven to 300 degrees F. Heat 2 tbsps. of the oil over medium-high heat in a large cast-iron skillet. Melt 2 tbsps. of the butter into the oil until it starts to bubble, and then add 1 of the breaded veal cutlets and cook until golden brown on both sides and cooked through, flipping once and moving the pan constantly, 3 to 4 minutes total. Transfer to

a baking sheet lined with a cooling rack, season with salt and pepper and keep warm in the oven. Cook the remaining cutlets, making sure to wipe out the pan and use new oil and butter each time. Keep adding the finished veal cutlets to the baking sheet in the oven as you cook them.

5. To serve, top the wiener schnitzel with the parsley and lemon wedges.
6. Serve and enjoy!

Oktoberfest Onion Pretzel Rolls

Ingredients:

2 tbsps. unsalted butter
2 cups diced yellow onions
1 tsp. kosher salt
1 cup warm water (105 to 115 degrees F)
1 package active dry yeast
2 3/4 cups bread flour, plus more for dusting
1 tsp. granulated sugar
2 tsps. vegetable oil, plus more for greasing
1/4 cup pretzel or coarse salt
1 tbsp. caraway seeds, lightly crushed
1/4 cup baking soda
German mustard, for serving, optional

Directions:

1. Melt the butter in a small skillet over medium heat. Add the onions and 1/2 tsp. of the salt and cook until softened and caramelized, 18 to 20 minutes. Transfer to a small bowl and cool completely.
2. Pour the water into the bowl of a stand mixer with the hook attachment and sprinkle in the yeast. Let the mixture rest until it bubbles, 4 to 6 minutes.
3. Sift together the flour, sugar and remaining 1/2 tsp. salt into a large bowl and stir to combine.
4. Add the flour mixture and caramelized onions into the mixer and mix on the lowest speed until the dough comes together.
5. Increase the speed to medium and mix until the dough is elastic and smooth, 6 to 8 minutes.
6. Grease a large mixing bowl with 1 tsp. of the oil. Form the dough into a ball and place it in the bowl, gently turning until coated. Cover with a clean, damp towel and let rest in

a warm place until the dough rises 1 1/2 times in size, 35 to 40 minutes.

7. Line a baking sheet with parchment paper and evenly coat it with the remaining oil. Set aside.

8. Transfer the dough to a clean, lightly-floured surface. Punch down the dough and knead until smooth and no longer sticky, 6 to 8 minutes. The dough should spring back when you lightly press it with a finger.

9. Divide the dough into 8 equal pieces, about 4 oz. each, and form into 4-inch-long rolls with slightly rounded, tapered ends.

10. Place the rolls on the prepared baking sheet, making sure there is enough room between each to allow it to double in size.

11. Cut three 1/4-inch-deep diagonal slashes across the top of each roll, then cover with a damp towel and set in a warm place to rise until the rolls almost double in volume, 20 to 25 minutes.

12. Place one rack on the very top shelf of the oven and another on the bottom shelf. Preheat the oven to 425 degrees F.

13. Stir together the pretzel salt and caraway seeds in a small bowl and set aside.

14. Line 1 baking sheet with a dry towel and another baking sheet with greased parchment or a silicone mat.

15. Bring 8 cups of water to a boil in a deep straight-sided skillet, and then stir in the baking soda.

16. Boil 4 of the rolls, flipping in the water, 1 minute, and then transfer to the towel-lined baking sheet using a slotted spoon. Repeat with the remaining rolls.

17. Let the rolls dry for 1 minute before transferring to the parchment-lined baking sheet and sprinkling with the caraway salt.

18. Bake the rolls on the top shelf of the oven until deep golden brown, 10 to 12 minutes, and then switch to the bottom shelf and continue baking until cooked through, 2 minutes longer.

19. Serve and enjoy!

Oktoberfest Beer Braised Brisket

Ingredients:

One 5-pound beef brisket
Kosher salt
Freshly ground black pepper
2 tbsps. canola oil
4 cups low-sodium beef stock
4 stalks celery, cut into 1-inch pieces
3 large carrots, cut into 1-inch pieces
2 bay leaves
2 large red onions, cut into 1-inch pieces
1 small bundle fresh thyme, tied together with kitchen twine
One 12-oz. bottle dark German beer

Directions:

1. Preheat the oven to 350 degrees F. Pat the brisket until very dry and sprinkle liberally with salt and pepper. Heat the oil in a large Dutch oven over medium-high heat, and then brown the meat well on all sides, 10 to 12 minutes. Transfer to a large plate and set aside.
2. Combine 1/4 cup of the beef stock, the celery, carrots, bay leaves, onions and thyme in the same Dutch oven and cook until the vegetables have started to brown and soften slightly, 4 to 6 minutes. Pour in the beer, bring to a boil and cook until reduced by half, 2 to 3 minutes. Return the brisket to the Dutch oven, and then pour in the remaining beef stock. The brisket should be at least halfway covered by the liquid.
3. Cover the pot and transfer to the oven for 3 hours 30 minutes. Remove the lid and cook uncovered for another 30 minutes. Let the brisket rest in the liquid in the pot for 20 minutes before transferring to a cutting board.
4. To serve, slice the brisket against the grain, place on a platter and ladle some braising liquid on top.

5. Serve and enjoy!

Oktoberfest Schupfnudeln (Fried Potato Dumplings)

Ingredients:

3 med. russet potatoes
Zest of 3 oranges, finely minced
1 cup granulated sugar
1 vanilla bean, scraped
1/2 cup all-purpose flour, plus extra for dusting
1/2 tsp. kosher salt
1 large egg, beaten
Vegetable oil, for frying

Directions:

1. Boil the potatoes until fork tender.
2. Drain in a colander and cool slightly.
3. Put the orange zest on a microwave-safe paper-towel-lined plate and microwave in 30-second intervals until the zest is dry and almost brittle, 3 to 4 minutes total.
4. Add zest, sugar and vanilla bean to a food processor and grind until the sugar is slightly powdery with bits of vanilla bean and orange zest throughout.
5. Pour into a large mixing bowl.
6. Peel and cut the potatoes into 1-inch chunks.
7. Press the potatoes through a potato ricer into a large mixing bowl.
8. Stir in the flour, salt and egg.
9. Knead well to form a smooth dough.
10. Turn out the dough onto a lightly-floured surface and roll into a 10-by-8-inch 1/2-inch-thick rectangle.
11. Cut the dough in half lengthwise using a bench scraper, and then cut across the dough widthwise into 1/2-inch sections to produce 34 rectangles.
12. Roll the rectangles into 6-inch-long dumplings with tapered ends using your hands.

13. Transfer to a parchment-lined flour-dusted baking sheet and let the dumplings rest at room temperature for 15 minutes.
14. Fill a large Dutch oven with 2 inches of oil and bring to 375 degrees F over medium-high heat.
15. Fry the dumplings in small batches until very golden brown and crispy, 4 to 5 minutes.
16. Transfer to a paper-towel-lined baking sheet to drain.
17. Toss the hot dumplings in the orange-vanilla sugar to coat.
18. Serve and enjoy!

Oktoberfest Duck Meatballs

Ingredients:

2 duck breasts
1 small yellow onion, finely chopped (about 1/2 cup)
2 tbsps. plain breadcrumbs
2 tbsps. milk
Kosher salt
Freshly ground black pepper
1 1/2 tsps. fresh thyme, chopped
1/2 tsp. dried juniper berries, ground in a spice grinder
2 1/2 tsps. Dijon mustard

Cherry Sauce Ingredients:

1 tsp. fresh thyme, chopped
1/3 cup shallot, diced
1 tbsp. Kirsch
One 12-oz. bag frozen cherries, thawed and halved, juice reserved
1/2 cup cherry jam
Kosher salt
Freshly ground black pepper

Directions:

1. Remove the skin from the duck breasts and cut the skin into 1/2-inch strips.
2. Cut the duck breasts into chunks.
3. Freeze duck chunks on a baking sheet for 30 minutes.
4. Heat a large skillet over medium heat.
5. Cook the duck skin until crispy and most of the fat has been rendered, 14 to 16 minutes, and then remove the skin from the pan and reserve for another use.
6. Pour the rendered fat into a small bowl, leaving about 1 tbsp. in the pan.
7. Add the onions to the skillet and cook until softened, 6 to 8 minutes.

8. Turn off the heat and stir in the breadcrumbs and milk to combine.
9. Prepare a meat grinder with the finest die.
10. Toss the duck breasts with 1 1/2 tsps. salt, 1/4 tsp. pepper, the thyme and juniper.
11. Run the seasoned duck through the meat grinder on medium speed into a large mixing bowl, working in batches.
12. Mix in the reserved onion and breadcrumb mixture and the mustard until just combined, being careful not to over-mix.
13. Spoon out tablespoonfuls of the duck mixture and roll into 24 meatballs. Place the meatballs onto a small baking sheet and refrigerate for 2 hours or up to overnight.

Cherry Sauce Directions:

1. Heat 1 tbsp. of the reserved duck fat in the same large skillet over medium heat.
2. Add the thyme and shallots and cook until softened, 4 to 6 minutes.
3. Stir in the Kirsch and frozen cherries along with their juice to combine and bring the mixture to a boil.
4. Continue cooking until the liquid is reduced by half, about 15 minutes, and then lower the heat to medium and whisk in the cherry jam.
5. Simmer for 2 minutes longer, and then season with salt and pepper.
6. Cover and set aside.
7. Heat 2 tbsps. of the reserved duck fat in a large nonstick skillet over medium heat. Add 12 meatballs to the skillet and cook until lightly browned on all sides, turning frequently, 6 to 8 minutes.
8. Transfer the meatballs to a large plate.
9. Heat another 2 tbsps. of the duck fat in the skillet and repeat with the remaining meatballs.
10. Bring the cherry sauce back to a simmer, uncovered, over medium heat.
11. Stir in the meatballs to combine and cook until warmed through and glazed with the sauce, 1 to 2 minutes.

12. Serve and enjoy!

Oktoberfest Jaeger Schnitzel

Gravy Ingredients:

8 oz. sliced bacon, cut into 1/4-inch pieces
1 yellow onion, chopped into 1/4-inch pieces
8 oz. cremini mushrooms, sliced 1/4-inch thick
1 tsp. fresh thyme, chopped
2 cups beef stock
1 tbsp. plus 1 tsp. all-purpose flour

Wiener Schnitzel Ingredients:

Four 5-oz. veal cutlets, pounded 1/8_inch thick (11"x 3")
Kosher salt
Freshly ground pepper
1 cup all-purpose flour
2 tbsps. German hot mustard
3 eggs
2 cups plain dried breadcrumbs
1/2 cup canola oil
1/2 cup unsalted butter
1/4 cup fresh flat-leaf parsley, roughly chopped, for garnish

Gravy Directions:

1. Cook the bacon in a large skillet over medium heat until crispy and most of the fat has been rendered, 10 to 12 minutes. Transfer to a paper-towel-lined plate to absorb any excess fat and set aside.
2. Add the onions to the pan and cook until softened, 4 to 6 minutes, and then stir in the mushrooms and thyme and cook until the mushrooms are just cooked through, 4 to 6 minutes longer.
3. Stir in 1/4 cup of the beef stock to combine, and then stir in the flour to combine and cook for 2 to 3 minutes.
4. Add the remaining stock and bring to a boil over medium-high heat, and then reduce to a simmer and cook, stirring

frequently, until the sauce is thickened to the consistency of gravy, 6 to 8 minutes.

5. Cover and set aside.

Wiener Schnitzel Directions:

1. Place each veal cutlet in between two pieces of plastic wrap. Pound each one using the spiky side of a meat mallet to tenderize it. Lightly season with salt and pepper.
2. Set up the breading station.
3. Whisk together the flour, 1/4 tsp. salt and 1/4 tsp. pepper in a shallow baking dish, and whisk together the mustard and eggs in another shallow baking dish.
4. Combine the breadcrumbs with 1/4 tsp. salt and 1/4 tsp. pepper in a third baking dish.
5. Dredge each veal cutlet first in the flour, then through the egg mixture, and lastly through the breadcrumbs. Transfer onto a baking sheet lined with a cooling rack and refrigerate for 15 minutes.
6. Preheat the oven to 300 degrees F.
7. Heat 2 tbsps. of the oil over medium-high heat in a large cast-iron skillet.
8. Melt 2 tbsps. of the butter into the oil until it starts to bubble, and then add 1 of the breaded veal cutlets and cook until golden brown on both sides and cooked through, flipping once and moving the pan constantly, 3 to 4 minutes total.
9. Transfer to a baking sheet lined with a cooling rack, season with salt and pepper and keep warm in the oven.
10. Cook the remaining cutlets, making sure to wipe out the pan and use new oil and butter each time.
11. Keep adding the finished veal cutlets to the baking sheet in the oven as you cook them.
12. Pour the gravy over the wiener Schnitzel.
13. Serve and enjoy!

Oktoberfest Fried Potatoes with Poached Eggs

Ingredients:

3-4 russet potatoes
8 oz. sliced smoked bacon
1/4 cup plus 3 tbsps. white distilled vinegar
2 tbsps. German mustard
Kosher salt
Freshly ground black pepper
3 tbsps. canola oil
1 large red onion, diced
6 eggs, at room temperature
1/4 cup fresh chives, chopped

Directions:

1. Fill a large saucepan with cold water, add the potatoes and bring to a boil over medium-high heat. Lower to a simmer and cook until a fork pierces through the potatoes with a bit of resistance, about 20 minutes. The potatoes should only be par-boiled at this point.
2. Drain, transfer to a small baking sheet, and freeze for 1 hour.
3. Cook the bacon in a large cast-iron skillet until crispy and most of the fat has been rendered, 10 to 12 minutes. Transfer to a paper-towel-lined plate and crumble.
4. Pour the bacon fat from the pan into a heatproof bowl and set aside.
5. Whisk together 3 tbsps. of the vinegar and the mustard in a small bowl. Slowly stream in 1/4 cup of the hot bacon fat, whisking until emulsified.
6. Season with salt and pepper.
7. Remove the potatoes from the freezer and cut into 1/2-inch cubes.

8. Preheat the oven to 400 degrees F. Pour about 1 1/2 inches of water and the remaining white distilled vinegar into a large straight-sided skillet and bring to a slow simmer.
9. Heat 3 tbsps. of the reserved bacon fat and the canola oil in the same skillet used for the bacon over medium heat.
10. Add the red onions and cook until softened, 4 to 6 minutes, and then add the potatoes. Season liberally with salt and black pepper and saute until the potatoes are just cooked through, stirring frequently, 4 to 6 minutes.
11. Turn the heat to medium high and continue cooking until the potatoes are browned and crispy, stirring frequently, 6 to 8 minutes longer. Transfer the potatoes into the oven while you poach the eggs.
12. Crack the eggs one at a time into a cup, and then carefully slide each into the simmering water. Cook until firm, turning occasionally with a slotted spoon, 3 to 5 minutes, and then transfer to a kitchen towel-lined plate with the slotted spoon. Sprinkle with salt and pepper.
13. Toss the potatoes with the mustard-bacon vinaigrette.
14. Serve topped with the poached eggs and garnished with the reserved bacon and chives.
15. Serve and enjoy!

German Creamed Spinach

Ingredients:

Two 10 oz. boxes frozen spinach, thawed
3 tbsps. unsalted butter
1 cup yellow onion, diced
Kosher salt
Freshly ground pepper
1 1/2 cups heavy cream
1/8 tsp. freshly grated nutmeg
2 cups grated aged Gouda cheese

Directions:

1. Strain the thawed spinach through a colander, and then wrap in a kitchen towel and squeeze out as much liquid as possible.
2. Melt the butter in a large straight-sided skillet over medium heat.
3. Cook the onions until softened, 6 to 8 minutes, and then season with salt and pepper.
4. Add the cream and nutmeg and cook until the cream is reduced by half, 2 to 3 minutes. Stir in the cheese until melted, and then mix in the spinach to combine.
5. Cover and cook over medium-low heat until the spinach is tender, 8 to 10 minutes, and then season with salt and pepper. Transfer to a bowl and serve immediately.
6. Serve and enjoy!

German Potato Salad

Ingredients:

1 pound fingerling potatoes
4 slices bacon
1/4 cup diced onion
1 tsp. minced garlic
2 tbsps. whole grain mustard
2 tbsps. apple cider vinegar
1/4 cup minced fresh parsley
Kosher salt
Freshly ground black pepper

Directions:

1. Boil the potatoes in salted water until fork tender.
2. Remove from the heat and allow to cool.
3. Cut the potatoes into 1/2-inch thick coins and set aside.
4. Cut the bacon into 1/2-inch pieces. In a heavy-bottomed sauté pan set over medium heat, cook the bacon until crispy, about 4 minutes.
5. Remove the bacon to a paper towel-lined plate.
6. In the same pan, add the onions and cook until soft, about 2 minutes.
7. Add the garlic and cook until fragrant, about 1 minute more.
8. Stir in the mustard and vinegar and scrape any browned bits from the bottom of the pan into the dressing.
9. Remove from the heat, gently stir in the potatoes and toss to coat.
10. Stir in the parsley and season with salt and pepper.
11. Serve and enjoy!

German Red Cabbage Soup

Ingredients:

1 tbsp. extra-virgin olive oil
6 slices smoky bacon, chopped
1 large onion, chopped
1 large carrot, peeled and chopped
1 1/2 tsps. caraway or cumin seed
1 apple (such as Braeburn or Northern Spy), finely chopped
1 small red cabbage, quartered, cored and sliced
Freshly ground black pepper
Freshly grated nutmeg

Cheesecloth Ingredients:

5 to 6 juniper berries
3 to 4 whole cloves
2 fresh bay leaves
Curl orange rind
1 small cinnamon stick
1/4 cup cider vinegar or wine vinegar
2 rounded tbsps. dark brown sugar
6 cups chicken stock
Kosher salt
Special equipment: Kitchen twine

Directions:

1. Heat a large soup pot over medium-high heat.
2. Add 1 tbsp. extra-virgin olive oil, and bacon.
3. Brown and crisp bacon and remove to a plate, draining off some fat but leave enough to lightly coat the bottom of the pot.
4. Add the onions, carrots, caraway, and apples, and stir a few minutes.
5. Wilt in the cabbage and season with black pepper and some freshly grated nutmeg.

6. Cover with the lid slightly ajar and wilt cabbage.
7. Fill the cheesecloth with the juniper berries, cloves, bay leaves, orange rind, and cinnamon, and use kitchen twine to tie it to the side of the pot.
8. Drop it into the pot and stir into the cabbage.
9. Add the vinegar, brown sugar, stock, and water, and bring the soup to a boil.
10. Reduce heat and simmer 1 to 1 1/2 hours, until cabbage is very tender and soup has thickened.
11. Stir the bacon bits back in, then add salt to taste.
12. Serve and enjoy!

German Twists

Ingredients:

1 (.25 oz.) pkg. active dry yeast
1/4 cup warm water
3 1/2 cups all-purpose flour
1 tsp. salt
1 cup butter, sliced
3/4 cup sour cream
1 large egg
2 large egg yolks
1 tsp. vanilla extract
1 cup white sugar, or as needed

Directions:

1. Sprinkle yeast over warm water in a bowl and let activate while you complete remaining steps.
2. Place flour and salt into a food processor and pulse once or twice to combine. Scatter butter slices over flour and process until butter is thoroughly mixed into the flour, about 1 minute.
3. Whisk yeast mixture, sour cream, egg, egg yolks, and vanilla extract together in a bowl; pour mixture into food processor.
4. Pulse several times, just until the dough starts to hold together and clean the sides of the bowl.
5. Remove dough and divide in half; form each half into a thick disk.
6. Wrap in plastic wrap, and refrigerate at least 2 hours.
7. For best texture, refrigerate overnight.
8. Preheat oven to 375 degrees F (190 degrees C).
9. Line several baking sheets with parchment paper.
10. Sprinkle a work surface generously with sugar and roll out one of the dough disks into an 8x16-inch rectangle.
11. Sprinkle dough with a generous amount of sugar.

12. Fold the dough over in thirds, letter-style, and roll out again; fold as before and roll out and fold a third time, sprinkling dough with sugar each time.
13. Finally, roll dough into a 4x14-inch rectangle, about 1/4 inch thick.
14. Repeat process with second dough disk.
15. Cut strips from the short side of the dough rectangles, making them 1/2 to 3/4 inch wide.
16. Place strips onto the parchment-lined baking sheets, twisting and slightly stretching them.
17. Form into horseshoe shapes.
18. Bake in the preheated oven until lightly golden brown, 12 to 15 minutes.
19. Cookies will puff up a bit to reveal delicate layers.
20. Allow to cool for about 5 minutes on sheets before transferring to wire cooling racks.
21. Serve and enjoy!

German Lebkuchen (Christmas Cookie)

Ingredients:

1 egg
3/4 cup brown sugar
1/2 cup honey
1/2 cup dark molasses
3 cups sifted all-purpose flour
1/2 tsp. baking soda
1 1/4 tsps. ground nutmeg
1 1/4 tsps. ground cinnamon
1/2 tsp. ground cloves
1/2 tsp. ground allspice
1/2 cup slivered almonds
1/2 cup candied mixed fruit peel, finely chopped
1 egg white, beaten
1 tbsp. lemon juice
1/2 tsp. lemon zest
1 1/2 cups sifted confectioners' sugar

Directions:

1. In a large bowl, beat the egg, brown sugar and honey until smooth.
2. Stir in the molasses.
3. Combine the flour, baking soda, nutmeg, cinnamon, cloves and allspice; stir into the molasses mixture.
4. Stir in the almonds and candied fruit peel.
5. Cover or wrap dough, and chill overnight.
6. Preheat the oven to 400 degrees F (200 degrees C).
7. Grease cookie sheets.
8. On a lightly floured surface, roll the dough out to 1/4 inch in thickness.
9. Cut into 2x3 inch rectangles.
10. Place cookies 1 1/2 inches apart onto cookie sheets.

11. Bake for 10 to 12 minutes in the preheated oven, until firm.
12. While still warm, brush the cookies with the lemon glaze.

Glaze Directions:

13. In a small bowl, stir together the egg white, lemon juice and lemon zest. Mix in the confectioners' sugar until smooth. Brush over cookies.
14. Serve and enjoy!

Oktoberfest German Honey Cookies

Ingredients:

1 cup white sugar
1 cup shortening
1 cup honey
2 eggs
1 tsp. vanilla extract
1 tsp. baking soda
4 cups all-purpose flour
1 tsp. ground ginger

Directions:

1. Preheat oven to 350 degrees F (180 degrees C).
2. In a saucepan over low heat, melt together sugar, shortening and honey.
3. Let cool.
4. Mix together eggs, vanilla, baking soda and ginger. Gradually add to cooled honey mixture.
5. Slowly add 4 cups of flour to mixture.
6. Stir until well blended.
7. Drop by teaspoonfuls onto cookie sheets about 2 inches apart.
8. Bake 12-15 minutes until golden brown.
9. Serve and enjoy!

Oktoberfest Cut Out Cookies

Ingredients:

1 cup butter, softened
2 cups brown sugar
2 eggs
1 tbsp. vanilla extract
4 cups all-purpose flour
1 tsp. baking soda
1 tsp. baking powder
1/2 tsp. salt

Directions:

1. In a large bowl, cream together the butter and brown sugar. Beat in the eggs and vanilla extract until well blended.
2. Combine the flour, baking soda, baking powder and salt; stir into the creamed mixture.
3. On a lightly floured surface, roll the dough out to 1/4 inch in thickness.
4. Cut into desired shapes with cookie cutters.
5. Place cookies 1 1/2 inches apart onto cookie sheets.
6. Bake for 8 to 10 minutes in the preheated oven.
7. Allow cookies to cool on baking sheet for 5 minutes before removing to a wire rack to cool completely.
8. Decorate with your favorite frostings or sprinkles if you like.
9. Serve and enjoy!

Oktuberfest German Chocolate Cake

Ingredients:

1/2 cup water
4 (1 oz.) squares German sweet chocolate
1 cup butter, softened
2 cups white sugar
4 egg yolks
1 tsp. vanilla extract
1 cup buttermilk
2 1/2 cups cake flour
1 tsp. baking soda
1/2 tsp. salt
4 egg whites
1 cup white sugar
1 cup evaporated milk
1/2 cup butter
3 egg yolks, beaten
1 1/3 cups flaked coconut
1 cup chopped pecans
1 tsp. vanilla extract
1/2 tsp. shortening
1 (1 oz.) square semisweet chocolate

Directions:

1. Preheat oven to 350 degrees F (175 degrees C).
2. Grease and flour 3 - 9 inch round pans.
3. Sift together the flour, baking soda and salt.
4. Set aside.
5. In a small saucepan, heat water and 4 oz. chocolate until melted. Remove from heat and allow to cool.
6. In a large bowl, cream 1 cup butter and 2 cups sugar until light and fluffy.
7. Beat in 4 egg yolks one at a time.

8. Blend in the melted chocolate mixture and vanilla. Beat in the flour mixture alternately with the buttermilk, mixing just until incorporated.
9. In a large glass or metal mixing bowl, beat egg whites until stiff peaks form.
10. Fold 1/3 of the whites into the batter, then quickly fold in remaining whites until no streaks remain.
11. Pour into 3 - 9 inch pans Bake in the preheated oven for 30 minutes, or until a toothpick inserted into the center of the cake comes out clean.
12. Allow to cool for 10 minutes in the pan, then turn out onto wire rack.

Filling Directions:

1. In a saucepan combine 1 cup sugar, evaporated milk, 1/2 cup butter, and 3 egg yolks.
2. Cook over low heat, stirring constantly until thickened.
3. Remove from heat.
4. Stir in coconut, pecans and vanilla.
5. Cool until thick enough to spread.
6. Spread filling between layers and on top of cake.
7. In a small saucepan, melt shortening and 1 oz. of chocolate.
8. Stir until smooth and drizzle down the sides of the cake.
9. Serve and enjoy!

Oktoberfest Sauerbraten

Ingredients:

3 pounds beef rump roast
2 large onions, chopped
1 cup red wine vinegar, or to taste
1 cup water
1 tbsp. salt
1 tbsp. ground black pepper
1 tbsp. white sugar
10 whole cloves, or more to taste
2 bay leaves, or more to taste
2 tbsps. all-purpose flour
Salt to taste
Ground black pepper to taste
2 tbsps. vegetable oil
10 gingersnap cookies, crumbled

Directions:

1. Place beef rump roast, onions, vinegar, water, 1 tbsp. salt, 1 tbsp. black pepper, sugar, cloves, and bay leaves in a large pot.
2. Cover and refrigerate for 2 to 3 days, turning meat daily.
3. Remove meat from marinade and pat dry with paper towels, reserving marinade.
4. Season flour to taste with salt and black pepper in a large bowl.
5. Sprinkle flour mixture over beef.
6. Heat vegetable oil in a large Dutch oven or pot over medium heat; cook beef until brown on all sides, about 10 minutes.
7. Pour reserved marinade over beef, cover, and reduce heat to medium-low.
8. Simmer until beef is tender, 3 1/2 to 4 hours.
9. Remove beef to a platter and slice.

10. Strain solids from remaining liquid and continue cooking over medium heat.
11. Add gingersnap cookies and simmer until gravy is thickened about 10 minutes.
12. Serve gravy over sliced beef.
13. Serve and enjoy!

German Gingersnaps

Ingredients:

1 cup white sugar
1/4 cup light molasses
1 egg
2 cups all-purpose flour
1/4 tsp. salt
2 tsps. baking soda
1 tsp. ground cinnamon
1 tsp. ground cloves
1/2 tsp. ground ginger
1/3 cup granulated sugar for decoration
3/4 cup shortening

Directions:

1. Preheat oven to 350 degrees (175 degrees C).
2. Cream together shortening and sugar. Mix in molasses and egg.
3. Stir in sifted flour, salt, soda, cinnamon, clove, and ginger.
4. Dough will be soft and a little sticky.
5. Mold into walnut-sized balls, and roll in sugar.
6. Place on greased cookie sheets.
7. Bake for 7 to 8 minutes.
8. Serve and enjoy!

Oktoberfest Hoernchen (Christmas Cookies)

Ingredients:

2 1/4 cups all-purpose flour
1 pinch salt
1/3 cup superfine sugar
1/3 cup ground almonds
2/3 cup butter
1 egg, beaten
1 tbsp. white wine
1 tbsp. rum
2 tsps. lemon zest
3 tbsps. butter, melted
1/2 cup fruit preserves, any flavor
1 egg yolk, beaten

Directions:

1. In a medium bowl, stir together the flour, salt, sugar and almonds.
2. Cut in the 2/3 cup butter until the mixture is crumbly.
3. Add egg, wine, rum and lemon zest.
4. Mix gently until well blended.
5. Adjust the flour if necessary to make a stiff dough.
6. On a lightly floured surface, knead the dough briefly, shape into a ball, wrap and chill for at least one hour or until firm.
7. Preheat oven to 350 degrees F (175 degrees C).
8. On a floured surface, roll the dough out to less than 1/4 inch in thickness.
9. Brush with melted butter and cut into triangles about three inches across. Place a dab of jam along one side of each triangle and roll up from the jam end to the point.
10. Seal with a dab of water if necessary.
11. Place pastry horn onto an ungreased cookie sheet and brush with beaten egg yolk.

12. Bake for 20 to 25 minutes in the preheated oven, until crisp and golden.
13. Dust with confectioners' sugar.
14. Serve and enjoy!

Oktuberfest Soft Pretzels

Ingredients:

1 1/2 cups warm water
1 tbsp. white sugar
5 tsps. active dry yeast
4 cups all-purpose flour
1/4 cup melted butter
1 tsp. coarse salt
1 egg, beaten
Coarse salt to taste

Directions:

1. Preheat oven to 425 degrees F (220 degrees C).
2. Mix water and sugar together in a bowl until sugar is dissolved; add yeast. Let mixture stand until the yeast softens and begins to form a creamy foam, about 5 minutes.
3. Whisk flour, butter, and salt together in a bowl until well mixed; add yeast mixture and stir with a fork until dough starts to cling. Turn dough onto a floured work surface and knead until smooth.
4. Cut dough into 15 equal pieces and roll each piece between your hands into rope shapes at least the thickness of a pencil. Twist dough into desired shapes and arrange on a baking sheet; brush with egg and sprinkle coarse salt over each.
5. Bake in the preheated oven until pretzels are browned and cooked through, 8 to 12 minutes.
6. Serve and enjoy!

German Beer Festival Kielbasa

Ingredients:

1 pound ground pork
8 oz. lean ground beef
2 tsps. minced garlic
1 tsp. freshly ground black pepper
1 tbsp. salt
1 tbsp. brown sugar
1/2 tsp. ground allspice
1 tsp. fresh marjoram
1/2 tsp. liquid smoke flavoring
12 sausage casings

Directions:

1. In a large bowl, combine pork, beef and garlic.
2. In a separate bowl, stir together black pepper, salt, brown sugar, ground allspice, marjoram and liquid smoke.
3. Combine mixtures and knead with hands to combine.
4. Fill casings with meat mixture and refrigerate overnight.
5. Boil or grill before serving.
6. Serve and enjoy!

Oktoberfest Uber-Braten Kielbasa and Sauerkraut Casserole

Ingredients:

1 (12 oz.) package kluski (egg) noodles
1/3 cup butter
1/3 cup all-purpose flour
1/2 tsp. dry mustard powder
1/4 tsp. ground black pepper
3 cups milk
3/4 cup shredded Cheddar cheese
2 cups sauerkraut, drained
1 (16 oz.) package kielbasa sausage, cubed
1/2 cup dry bread crumbs
1/4 cup shredded Cheddar cheese

Directions:

1. Preheat oven to 375 degrees F (190 degrees C).
2. Bring a large pot of lightly salted water to a boil.
3. Cook kluski noodles in the boiling water, stirring occasionally until cooked through but firm to the bite, about 8 minutes.
4. Drain and set aside.
5. Melt butter in a large pot over medium heat.
6. Whisk in flour, dry mustard, and black pepper; cook until smooth, about 2 minutes.
7. Whisk in milk, a little at a time, and bring white sauce to a boil. Cook for 1 minute, whisking constantly, to make a smooth, thick sauce.
8. Whisk 3/4 cup Cheddar cheese into sauce until melted.
9. Stir kluski noodles, sauerkraut, and kielbasa sausage into the sauce and transfer to a 3-quart casserole dish.
10. Mix bread crumbs with 1/4 cup Cheddar cheese in a bowl and sprinkle over the casserole.

11. Bake in the preheated oven until casserole is heated through, about 20 minutes.
12. Serve and enjoy!

Oktoberfest Cucumber Slices With Dill

Ingredients:

4 lrg. cucumbers, sliced
1 onion, thinly sliced
1 tbsp. dried dill weed
1 cup white sugar
1/2 cup white vinegar
1/2 cup water
1 tsp. salt

Directions:

1. In a large serving bowl, combine cucumbers, onions and dill.
2. In a medium size bowl combine sugar, vinegar, water and salt; stir until the sugar dissolves.
3. Pour the liquid mixture over the cucumber mixture.
4. Cover and refrigerate at least 2 hours before serving.
5. Serve and enjoy!

Oktoberfest Bierocks (Meat Pockets)

Ingredients:

2 cups warm water
2 (.25 oz.) packages active dry yeast
1/2 cup white sugar
1/4 cup margarine, softened
1 egg
2 tsps. salt
7 cups all-purpose flour
1 lb. lean ground beef
1 cup chopped onion
6 cups shredded cabbage
1 tsp. salt 1 tsp. black pepper
1/4 cup melted butter

Directions:

1. Prepare dough: In a large bowl, dissolve yeast in warm water. Let stand until creamy, about 10 minutes.
2. Mix in sugar, margarine, egg, salt and 1/2 of the flour.
3. Beat until smooth; add remaining flour until dough pulls together.
4. Place in oiled bowl.
5. Cover with foil and let it rise for 1 hour.
6. In a large heavy skillet, brown meat.
7. Add onion, cabbage, salt and simmer 30 minutes.
8. Cool until lukewarm.
9. Preheat oven to 350 degrees F (175 degrees C.).
10. Coat a cookie sheet with non-stick spray.
11. Punch down dough and divide into 20 pieces.
12. Spread each piece of dough out on an un-floured surface and fill with approximately 2 tbsps. filling. fold dough over and seal edges.
13. Place on prepared cookie sheet and let rise for 1 hour.

14. Bake in the preheated oven for 25 minutes, or until golden brown.
15. Brush with butter.
16. Serve and enjoy!

Bavarian Kaes-Spaetzle (Egg Noodles)

Ingredients:

3 eggs
1 3/4 cups all-purpose flour
1/2 tsp. salt
1 tbsp. vegetable oil
1/2 cup water
1/4 cup vegetable oil
2 onions, halved and sliced
1 tbsp. vinegar
1 tsp. chopped fresh parsley, for garnish

Directions:

1. In a large bowl, combine eggs, flour, salt, 1 tbsp. oil, and 1/2 cup water.
2. Mix until smooth, then let rest for 10 minutes.
3. Heat 1/4 cup oil in a skillet over medium heat.
4. Sauté onion slices until golden brown; set aside.
5. Preheat oven to 300 degrees F (150 degrees C).
6. Bring a large pot of lightly salted water to a boil.
7. Place 1/3 of the dough into a spaetzle maker or coarse sieve or colander.
8. Let dough drop into boiling water.
9. Boil until spaetzle rises to the top, then transfer to a 9 inch casserole dish with a slotted spoon.
10. Cover with 1/3 of the cheese.
11. Repeat layers with remaining spaetzle and cheese.
12. Spoon fried onions over top.
13. Bake in preheated oven for 15 minutes, or until cheese is thoroughly melted.
14. Sprinkle with 1 or 2 tbsps. vinegar, and sprinkle with chopped parsley.
15. Serve and enjoy!

German Rouladen (Beef Olive)

Ingredients:

1 1/2 pounds flank steak
German stone ground mustard, to taste
1/2 pound thick sliced bacon
2 large onions, sliced
1 (16 oz.) jar dill pickle slices
2 tbsps. butter
2 1/2 cups water
1 cube beef bouillon

Directions:

1. Cut the flank steak into thin filets; about 1/4 inch thick and 3 inches wide.
2. Generously spread one side of each filet with mustard to taste.
3. Place bacon, onions and pickle slices on each filet and form into a roll.
4. Use string or toothpicks to hold the roll together.
5. Heat a skillet over medium heat and melt butter.
6. Place the rolls in the butter and saute until browned.
7. Pour in 2 1/2 cups of water and add the bouillon cube; stirring to dissolve the bouillon cube.
8. Simmer the rolls for about an hour.
9. Serve and enjoy!

Oktuberfest Potato Leek Soup

Ingredients:

1 cup chopped onion
1/2 cup butter
1 cup chopped leeks
8 potatoes, peeled and sliced
6 cups water
1/2 tsp. fresh thyme
1 ham bone
1 cup heavy cream
Salt and pepper to taste

Directions:

1. In a large pot over medium heat, cook onions in butter until translucent.
2. Stir in leeks, potatoes, water, thyme and the ham bone.
3. Bring to a boil, then reduce heat, cover and simmer until potatoes are tender, 20 to 30 minutes.
4. Remove ham bone and puree soup with a blender or food processor.
5. Return to pot, stir in cream, salt and pepper, heat through and serve.

Ocotoberfest Boiled Potatoes

Ingredients:

2 1/4 lbs. potatoes (such as Yukon gold), scrubbed, eyes removed
1 pinch salt
1/3 cup chopped fresh parsley

Directions:

1. Place potatoes in a large pot and cover with salted water.
2. Bring to a boil.
3. Reduce heat to medium-low and simmer until tender, about 20 minutes.
4. Drain.
5. Sprinkle on parsley.
6. Serve and enjoy!

Oktoberfest Semmelknoedel (Bread Dumplings)

Ingredients:

1 loaf stale French bread, cut into 1 inch cubes
1 cup milk
2 tbsps. butter
1 onion, finely chopped
1 tbsp. fresh parsley, chopped
2 eggs
1/2 tsp. salt
1 pinch ground black pepper
1/2 cup dry bread crumbs

Directions:

1. Place the bread cubes into a large bowl.
2. Heat the milk until it starts to bubble at the edges, then pour it over the bread cubes.
3. Stir briefly to coat the bread.
4. Let soak for 15 minutes.
5. Melt the butter in a skillet over medium heat.
6. Add the onions; cook and stir until tender. Stir in the parsley, and remove from the heat. Mix into the bowl with the bread along with the eggs, salt and pepper.
7. Use your hands, squeezing the dough through your fingers until it is smooth and sticky.
8. Bring a large pot of lightly salted water to a boil.
9. The water should be at least 3 or 4 inches deep.
10. When the water is boiling, make a test dumpling about the size of a small orange or tangerine, by patting and cupping between wet hands.
11. Gently drop into the boiling water. If it falls apart, the dough is too wet.
12. If too wet, stir some bread crumbs into the rest of the dumpling batter.

13. Form the remaining dough into large dumplings, and carefully drop into the boiling water.
14. Simmer for 20 minutes, then remove to a serving plate with a large slotted spoon.
15. Serve and enjoy!

Oktoberfest Beer Cheese Dip

Ingredients:

3/4 (8 oz.) package cream cheese
10 oz. processed cheese (such as Velveeta or American cheese), cubed
1 (12 fl. oz.) bottle beer, room temperature
4 slices smoked Gouda cheese
4 slices mozzarella cheese
4 slices smoked provolone cheese
1 tbsp. Worcestershire sauce
1 tbsp. brown sugar
1 tbsp. prepared horseradish, or to taste
3 cloves garlic
2 tsps. dry mustard
Salt
ground black pepper to taste

Directions:

1. Heat cream cheese and processed cheese together in a sauce pan over low heat until melted, 5 to 10 minutes.
2. Slowly stir beer into cheese mixture until thoroughly mixed.
3. Add Gouda cheese, mozzarella cheese, and provolone cheese to beer-cheese mixture, stirring continually until smooth, 5 to 10 minutes.
4. Stir Worcestershire sauce, brown sugar, horseradish, garlic, mustard, salt, and pepper into cheese mixture until well mixed and heated through, about 10 more minutes.
5. Great with German pretzels for Oktoberfest!
6. Serve and enjoy!

Oktoberfest Red Cabbage with Apples

Ingredients:

3 tbsps. coconut oil, or as needed
4 slices bacon, chopped
1 small onion, chopped
2 cloves garlic, minced, or to taste
1 head red cabbage, chopped
1/2 cup apple cider vinegar
1/4 cup brown sugar
2 cooking apples (such as Cortland or Gala) peeled and chopped
Salt
Ground black pepper to taste

Directions:

1. Heat coconut oil over medium heat in a large skillet; cook and stir bacon, onion, and garlic until fragrant, about 5 minutes.
2. Stir cabbage into bacon mixture and toss to coat with oil.
3. Cover skillet, reduce the heat, and cook, stirring occasionally, until cabbage begins to soften, about 10 minutes.
4. Stir cider vinegar and brown sugar together in a bowl.
5. Pour over cabbage mixture.
6. Stir apples into cabbage mixture; cover and cook, stirring occasionally, until most of the liquid has evaporated and cabbage is tender, about 35 minutes.
7. Remove pan from heat and allow cabbage mixture to stand, covered, for about 5 minutes; season with salt and pepper.
8. Serve and enjoy!

German Zwiebelkuchen (Onion Pie)

Ingredients:

4 cups all-purpose flour
1 tsp. salt
1 (.25 oz.) pkg. active dry yeast
2 tbsps. olive oil
1 cup lukewarm water

Filling Ingredients:

1/4 cup butter
2 1/4 pounds onions, cut into rings
1 tsp. salt
2 cups sour cream
1 cup milk
4 eggs
Ground black pepper to taste
1 pinch caraway seeds

Directions:

1. Mix flour, 1 tsp. salt, and yeast in a large bowl.
2. Stir in olive oil and about 3/4 cup water until mixture comes together in a ball of dough.
3. Turn dough out on a lightly floured surface.
4. Gradually add remaining 1/4 cup water while kneading dough; continue kneading until smooth and elastic, about 10 minutes.
5. Place dough in a large lightly-oiled bowl and turn to coat.
6. Cover with a towel and let rise in a warm place , about 30 minutes.
7. Melt butter in a large skillet over medium heat.

8. Cook and stir onions and 1 tsp. salt until tender and translucent, about 30 minutes; stir often so onions do not brown.
9. Remove from heat and allow to cool.
10. Preheat oven to 375 degrees F (190 degrees C).
11. Grease a baking sheet.
12. Roll dough out on a floured surface to create a thin crust; transfer dough to prepared baking sheet.
13. Poke several holes in the dough with a fork and roll edges up slightly to create a rim.
14. Spread cooled onions over crust.
15. Whisk sour cream, milk, eggs, and ground black pepper in a bowl; pour over onions.
16. Sprinkle with caraway seeds.
17. Bake until golden brown and eggs are set, 30 to 45 minutes.
18. Serve and enjoy!

German Currywurst

Ingredients:

3 (15 oz.) cans tomato sauce
1 pound kielbasa
2 tbsps. chili sauce
1/2 tsp. onion salt
1 tbsp. white sugar
1 tsp. ground black pepper
1 pinch paprika
Curry powder to taste

Directions:

1. Preheat oven to Broil or heat the grill.
2. Pour tomato sauce into a large saucepan.
3. Stir in the chili sauce, onion salt, sugar and pepper.
4. Let simmer over medium heat, occasionally stirring and bring to a gentle boil.
5. Reduce heat to low once boiling.
6. Simmer another 5 minutes.
7. Broil or grill kielbasa sausage for 3 to 4 minutes each side, or until cooked through.
8. Slice into pieces 1/4 inch to 1/2 inch thick.
9. Pour tomato sauce mixture over sausage.
10. Sprinkle all with paprika and curry powder.
11. Serve and enjoy!

German Chicken

Ingredients:

skinless, boneless chicken breast halves
1 cup barbecue sauce
22 oz. sauerkraut

Directions:

1. Preheat oven to 350 degrees F (175 degrees C).
2. In a 9x13 inch baking dish, place the sauerkraut in a single layer.
3. Place the chicken breasts on top of the sauerkraut.
4. Pour the barbecue sauce over the chicken.
5. Cover and bake for 30 minutes or until the chicken is cooked and the juices run clear.
6. Serve and enjoy!

German Rice

Ingredients:

1/4 cup olive oil
1 1/2 lbs. fresh bratwurst links, casings removed
1 onion, halved and thinly sliced into half rings
1 tsp. minced garlic
2 tsps. fennel seed
1 can (14.5 oz.) Bavarian-style sauerkraut, undrained
3 cups uncooked white rice
1 tbsp. chicken soup base (paste)
6 cups water
1 tsp. ground black pepper
1/4 cup raisins

Directions:

1. In a large pot over medium heat, heat the olive oil, and cook the skinned bratwurst until browned, breaking the sausage up into chunks as it cooks, about 10 minutes.
2. Stir in the onions and garlic, and cook until the onions are translucent, about 5 more minutes.
3. Mix in fennel seed and sauerkraut with juice, and allow the mixture to pan-fry for 2 minutes without stirring.
4. Mix in the rice and soup base, and stir until the rice is colored and the soup base is incorporated, about 2 more minutes.
5. Stir in water, black pepper, and raisins, and bring to a boil; cook for 5 minutes, stirring frequently.
6. Reduce heat to a simmer, and cook until rice is tender and almost all the water has absorbed, about 30 minutes.
7. Serve and enjoy!

Oktoberfest Pork Shank

Ingredients:

2-3 pounds pork shank
Seasoning
2 tbsps.   caraway seeds
1/2 head garlic (about six cloves)
Salt and pepper, the same amount used to season soup

Directions:

1. Boil hind pork shank in a pot of water with caraway seeds, garlic, salt and pepper, covered for one hour.
2. Use just enough water to submerge the shank in the pot you are using, and season water sufficiently so you don't need to season the meat again after cooking.
3. Retain the water for stock.
4. After one hour, let shank cool down to room temperature.
5. Cut skin horizontally, approximately 1/2 inch apart, and roast at 375 degrees for 90 minutes.
6. Use some of the stock in the bottom of the pan.
7. Raise temperature to 425 degrees F and crisp skin approximately 20 minutes.
8. To be traditional, serve it on a wooden platter with sauerkraut, country bread, pickles, horseradish and Bavarian mustard.
9. Serve and enjoy!

Oktoberfest Sausage and Sauerkraut Fritter

Ingredients:

1 bag fresh sauerkraut, drained
1 large   smoked Kielbasa sausage
4 slices thick-cut smoked bacon
2 tbsps. spicy mustard
1 cup Gruyere
8 eggs
1 cup breadcrumbs
For the breading:
3 cups flour
1 tsp. salt
1/2 tsp. black pepper
3 cups breadcrumbs

Dipping Sauce Ingredients:

1 cup mayonnaise
2 tbsps. honey
1/2 cup whole grain mustard

Directions:

1. Cut the bacon and sausage into small pieces.
2. Heat a medium sized frying pan on medium heat.
3. Add the bacon and sausage and cook for 4-5 minutes or until the bacon is crispy.
4. Remove from the heat and let cool completely.
5. Retain the bacon fat that remains in the pan and add it to the mixture to add flavor.
6. In a large mixing bowl, mix together the drained sauerkraut, mustard, breadcrumbs, 6 eggs and cheese.
7. When the bacon and sausage is cool, add it to the sauerkraut mixture and mix well.

8. Add a little more breadcrumbs to form a nice tight mixture.
9. Take three bowls, large enough to fit a few of the fritters into, and keep them separate.
10. Add the flour, salt, and pepper to one bowl, 2 beaten eggs to the second bowl and the breadcrumbs to the third bowl, keeping bowls in this order.
11. Take a few of the fritters, place in flour, and roll them around to coat well.
12. Next, dip the fritters into the egg, coating all sides, then to the bowl with the breadcrumbs.
13. Roll them in the breadcrumbs and place on a plate while you do the others.
14. Once you get all of them breaded you should place them in the refrigerator for at least in hour until they are very cold.
15. Using a large Dutch oven or small stockpot, heat up the oil to 350 degrees F.
16. Add the fritters one at a time.
17. Fry the fritters in the oil for about 5 - 6 minutes.
18. Using a slotted spoon, carefully remove them and place on a plate lined with a paper towel.
19. Continue to fry them until all of them are done.

Dipping Sauce Directions:

1. In a small mixing bowl, combine the mayonnaise, honey, and mustard and mix well.
2. Serve and enjoy!

Oktoberfest Sauerkraut

Ingredients:

1 head of cabbage
1 1/2 tbsps. salt

Directions:

1. Remove the outer leaves of your head of cabbage, and any underlying leaves that may be brown or damaged.
2. Cut the head of cabbage into quarters.
3. Remove the core and finely slice with a knife or mandolin.
4. Place the shredded cabbage into a glass or ceramic dish (not metal).
5. Add the salt at a ratio of one tbsp. of salt to one pound of cabbage and toss to evenly coat.
6. Cover with a kitchen towel or plastic wrap to keep debris out but do not seal.
7. After about an hour you will see that the cabbage will begin to wilt and release moisture, creating a liquid.
8. Keep the cabbage submerged by using a plate with a weight on top (like another glass bowl) to keep it under the liquid.
9. Place in a cool area and check after 2 days.
10. Skim the top of the liquid and discard the scum.
11. Use the plate to cover again.
12. After 4 more days, taste for doneness.
13. Refrigerate when done.
14. Serve and enjoy!

Oktoberfest Potato Pancakes

Ingredients:

4 baking potatoes
3/4 cup finely chopped onion
1 egg, beaten
1/4 cup all-purpose flour
1 tsp. baking powder
1/2 tsp. salt
1/4 tsp. black pepper
1/4 cup vegetable oil

Directions:

1. Coarsely grate the potatoes and put them and the onion in a strainer.
2. Press down with the back of a large spoon to extract excess moisture.
3. If they're still watery, wrap them in a clean dish towel and squeeze to extract moisture.
4. In a large bowl, combine potatoes, onion, and egg; mix well.
5. Gradually add flour, baking powder, salt, and pepper; mix well.
6. In a large skillet over medium heat, heat 1/4 inch oil.
7. Using about 1/3 cup of batter per pancake, add batter to the hot oil, being careful not to crowd the pan.
8. Fry 3 to 4 minutes or until golden; turn and fry an additional 3 to 4 minutes, or until cooked through. Add more oil as needed until all batter is used. Drain on paper towels and serve hot.

Oktoberfest Mustardy Cabbage

Ingredients:

1 tbsp. vegetable oil
4 slices bacon, chopped
1 cup chopped onion
1/2 head green cabbage, shredded
1 apple, cored and chopped
1/2 tsp. salt
1/4 tsp. black pepper
1/4 cup heavy cream
2 tbsps. whole grain mustard

Directions:

1. In a large skillet over medium-high heat, add oil, bacon, and onion and cook 6 to 8 minutes, or until bacon is crisp and onion starts to brown.
2. Add the cabbage, apple, salt, and pepper and continue cooking 8 to 10 minutes, or until cabbage is wilted.
3. Stir in cream and mustard and cook 2 to 3 minutes, or until heated through.

Oktoberfest Beer-Basted Sausage

Ingredients:

2 tbsps. canola oil
3 onions, peeled, quartered and sliced very thin
1/8 tsp. salt
1/8 tsp. black pepper
2 tbsps. spicy brown mustard
1 (1-pound) package bratwurst (6 to 8 sausages)
1/2 cup beer

Directions:

1. In a large skillet over medium-low heat, heat oil
2. Add onions and saute 10 minutes, or until tender and beginning to brown, stirring often.
3. Season onions with salt and pepper then stir in mustard.
4. Add bratwurst and cook 10 to 12 minutes, or until sausages are no longer pink in center.
5. Stir in the beer and simmer 2 to 3 minutes. Serve bratwurst with the onions.

Oktoberfest Apple Strudel

Ingredients:

1 sheet (from a 1.25-ounce package) frozen puff pastry, thawed
1/3 cup sugar
2 tsps. ground cinnamon
1 (20-ounce) can sliced apples, drained
1/3 cup raisins
1 egg, beaten

Directions:

1. Preheat oven to 400 degrees F.
2. Place pastry on a baking sheet and unfold.
3. In a medium bowl, combine sugar and cinnamon; mix well.
4. Reserve 2 tsps. sugar mixture.
5. Add apples and raisins to remaining mixture.
6. Mix well. Let sit about 2 minutes.
7. Drain off any excess liquid.
8. Spoon mixture down center of dough.
9. Cut slits in dough 1 inch apart lengthwise down each side of filling. Brush each 1-inch dough strip with beaten egg and crisscross strips over filling. Brush top of pastry with remaining egg and sprinkle with reserved sugar mixture.
10. Bake 20 to 25 minutes, or until golden.
11. Serve warm, or allow to cool before serving.

Oktoberfest Cherry Kuchen Bars

Ingredients:

1/2 cup butter, softened
1/2 cup shortening
1 1/2 cups sugar
3 eggs
1 tsp. vanilla extract
3 cups all-purpose flour
1 1/2 tsps. baking powder
1/2 tsp. salt
1 (21-oz.) can cherry pie filling

Directions:

1. Preheat oven to 350 degrees F.
2. In a large bowl, beat butter, shortening, and sugar until creamy.
3. Add eggs and vanilla; mix well.
4. In a medium bowl, combine flour, baking powder, and salt.
5. Slowly beat flour mixture into butter mixture until well combined.
6. Reserve 1-1/2 cups of dough; set aside.
7. Spread remaining dough in a 15- x 10- x 1-inch baking sheet.
8. Bake 10 minutes. Remove from oven and spread pie filling over crust.
9. Spoon reserved dough in small mounds on top of pie filling.
10. Continue baking 25 to 30 minutes, or until top is lightly golden. Let cool, then cut into squares.

Oktoberfest German Stuffing

Ingredients:

8 cups stale or lightly toasted rye bread with seeds, and cut into cubes
1/2 cup butter
2 celery stalks, chopped
1 carrot, peeled and chopped
1 cup chopped onion
1 apple, peeled, cored, and chopped
1 tsp. salt
1/4 tsp. black pepper
1 3/4 cups chicken broth, warmed
1 pound fresh sauerkraut, rinsed and drained
5 slices crispy cooked bacon, crumbled

Directions:

1. Preheat oven to 375 degrees F.
2. Coat an 8-inch square baking dish with cooking spray.
3. Place bread cubes in a large bowl; set aside.
4. In a large skillet over medium-high heat, melt butter.
5. Add celery, carrot, and onion and cook 5 minutes. Add apple, salt, and pepper and continue cooking 4 to 5 minutes, or until vegetables are tender.
6. Pour mixture over bread cubes. Add broth, sauerkraut, and bacon, and mix gently until well combined. Spoon stuffing into baking dish.
7. Cover and bake 20 minutes.
8. Uncover and bake an additional 15 to 20 minutes, or until heated through.

About the Author

Laura Sommers is **The Recipe Lady!**

She is the #1 Best Selling Author of over 80 recipe books.

She is a loving wife and mother who lives on a small farm in Baltimore County, Maryland and has a passion for all things domestic especially when it comes to saving money. She has a profitable eBay business and is a couponing addict. Follow her tips and tricks to learn how to make delicious meals on a budget, save money or to learn the latest life hack!

Visit her Amazon Author Page to see her latest books:

amazon.com/author/laurasommers

Visit the Recipe Lady's blog for even more great recipes and to learn which books are **FREE** for download each week:

http://the-recipe-lady.blogspot.com/

Other books in This Series

- **Best Traditional Irish Recipes for St. Patrick's Day**

- **Super Awesome Traditional Maryland Recipes**

- **Super Awesome Traditional Philadelphia Recipes**

- **Authentic Traditional Pennsylvania Dutch Amish and Mennonite Recipes**

- **Authentic Traditional Memphis, Tennessee Recipes**

- **Traditional Vermont Recipes**

- **Traditional Kentucky Recipes**

- **Best Traditional Cajun and Creole Recipes from New Orleans**

May all of your meals be a banquet
with good friends and good food.

Printed in Great Britain
by Amazon